THE SUPER BOWL

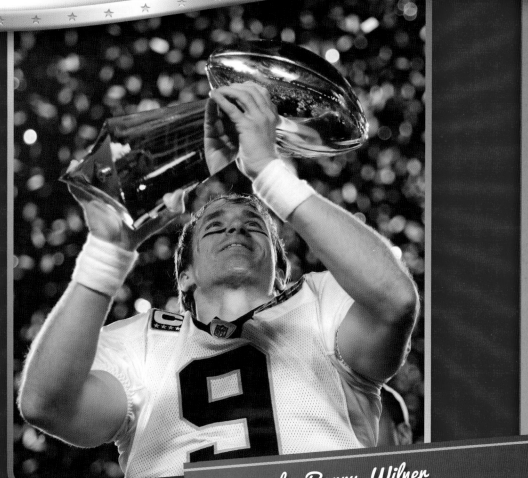

by Barry Wilner

Published by ABDO Publishing Company, PO Box 398166, Minneapolis, MN 55439. Copyright © 2013 by Abdo Consulting Group, Inc. International copyrights reserved in all countries. No part of this book may be reproduced in any form without written permission from the publisher. SportsZone™ is a trademark and logo of ABDO Publishing Company.

Printed in the United States of America,
North Mankato, Minnesota
102012
032014

 THIS BOOK CONTAINS AT LEAST 10% RECYCLED MATERIALS.

Editor: Chrös McDougall
Series Designer: Craig Hinton

Photo Credits: Paul Spinelli/AP Images, Cover, 35, 47, 49, 58 (bottom); David J. Phillip/AP Images, Title, 51; NFL Photos/AP Images, 5, 11, 13, 21, 23, 43, 58 (top, left), 59 (top); AP Images, 9, 17, 27, 29, 60 (bottom); Bettmann/Corbis/AP Images, 19; Dallas Morning News/Phil Huber/AP Images, 32; Phil Sandlin/AP Images, 37; Tom DiPace/AP Images, 39, 58 (top, right); Boulder Daily Camera/Cliff Grassmick/AP Images, 45; Scott A. Miller/AP Images, 55, 59 (bottom, left); Pat Semansky/AP Images, 57, 59 (bottom, right); Kevin Terrell/AP Images, 60 (top); Dough Mills/AP Images, 60 (center)

Cataloging-in-Publication Data
Wilner, Barry.
The Super Bowl / Barry Wilner.
  p. cm. -- (Sports' great championships)
Includes bibliographical references and index.
ISBN 978-1-61783-673-2
1. Football--History--Juvenile literature. 2. Super Bowl (Football game)--History--Juvenile literature. I. Title.
796.332/648--dc22

                                                              2012946244

TABLE OF CONTENTS

The Guarantee

There was no doubt about what would happen on January 12, 1969. The Baltimore Colts were going to stomp all over the New York Jets in Super Bowl III.

Baltimore had won the National Football League (NFL). At the time, the NFL was believed to be the stronger of the two professional football leagues. The NFL's Green Bay Packers had easily won the first two Super Bowls over their American Football League (AFL) opponents. Going into Super Bowl III, the Colts were considered superior to the AFL-champion

Tackle Bob Vogel and the Baltimore Colts came into Super Bowl III as heavy favorites over the AFL's New York Jets.

Jets in every way. The general belief was simple: The NFL was the better league, and the Colts were its top team by far.

Baltimore had finished 13–1 in the regular season. Then it rolled through the playoffs. The Jets, meanwhile, were less established. They finished 11–3 in the upstart AFL and survived a close game to make the Super Bowl. The betting odds made clear what many people already believed: The Colts were 17-point favorites.

No Worries

New York's charismatic quarterback Joe Namath had become known as "Broadway Joe." Fans loved him. He had become one of the biggest stars in the AFL. At one point, Namath questioned The Colts' defensive unit. To be sure, this was a defense that gave up just 144 points that season. The Jets, meanwhile, gave up 280.

As it turned out, Broadway Joe did not think much of Baltimore's offense or defense. The more he looked at film, the more he was convinced the Jets would win. And not only that, Namath became convinced they would win easily.

Namath and Colts quarterback Earl Morrall were honored at a banquet a few days before the Super Bowl. At one point, according to Namath, a man got up and yelled.

"Hey Namath," the Jets quarterback recalled the man saying, "the Colts are going to kick your [rear end]!"

"We'd been hearing a lot of that," Namath said later. "So I said, 'I've got news for you. We're going to win the game. I guarantee it.'"

Now Namath had really done it. It was wild enough that he doubted the Colts' greatness. But so far he had only shared his feelings with other Jets players. Now he had told the world.

He Said What?

Namath did not think much about his guarantee until the next day. Some of his teammates came by. They were not exactly happy that Namath had riled up the Colts.

Guard Dave Herman was about to play a key role in the Super Bowl. He would switch to tackle in a surprise move so he could block

Bubba Smith, Baltimore's star defensive end and pass rusher. Now Herman was mad. He told Namath it was tough enough going up against Smith without him being mad. Now everyone wearing Baltimore blue would be angry—and out to prove a point.

Jets coach Weeb Ewbank had led the Colts to NFL titles in 1958 and 1959, before the Super Bowl existed. He was not thrilled with Namath, either. Ewbank indeed wanted his quarterback and everyone else on the team thinking they could win. The last thing he wanted, though, was any of the Jets laying down such a bold challenge.

"I think it's fair to say Weeb wasn't too happy," Namath said, laughing. "He didn't see any value in saying anything."

Namath clearly did. After all, this was Broadway Joe. So now, Namath and the Jets had to back up his prediction.

Game Time

Jets star receiver Don Maynard had a hamstring injury. The team knew he would not be too useful. The hope was that Maynard could run one, maybe two deep routes all game.

The Jets sent Maynard deep on their second series. Namath threw a long pass that was incomplete. But Maynard had gotten free behind the defensive backs. From then on, the Colts paid extra attention to Maynard.

New York Jets quarterback Joe Namath hands off to running back Matt Snell during Super Bowl III against the Baltimore Colts.

That meant the Colts were paying less attention to the other Jets receivers. George Sauer now had single coverage all over the field. Namath took advantage. Sauer wound up with eight catches for 133 yards. Matt Snell caught four passes, Bill Mathis had three receptions, and tight end Pete Lammons had two. Maynard never caught a pass.

Snell's four-yard touchdown run in the second quarter gave the Jets a 7–0 lead. It marked the first time an AFL team had led in a Super Bowl. Meanwhile, Baltimore's blitzes were not working. The offense was not doing much, either.

The Chiefs

The Jets' win was not a fluke for the AFL. One year later in Super Bowl IV, the AFL's Kansas City Chiefs played the NFL-champion Minnesota Vikings. Again the NFL team was heavily favored. But once again the AFL team came out on top. The Chiefs won 23–7. Soon nobody was talking about the AFL as the weaker league.

The one true Colts scoring chance in the first half came on a trick play. Morrall did not see a wide-open Jimmy Orr on the play, however. So he threw to the other side of the field and the pass was picked off by Jets defensive back Jim Hudson.

At halftime, Colts coach Don Shula begged his players to stop making mistakes. They were playing nothing like they had all season. Ewbank told the Jets to just keep on doing what they were doing.

And they did. Two drives led to field goals by Jim Turner. The Jets had a 13–0 lead through three quarters. Another field goal made it 16–0. Shula replaced Morrall with future Hall of Fame quarterback Johnny Unitas late in the game. Unitas led the Colts to a touchdown. But Baltimore could not catch up.

In an iconic photo from Super Bowl III, New York Jets quarterback Joe Namath runs off the field following his team's surprising win over the Baltimore Colts.

Most importantly, the AFL had caught up to the NFL. Years later, New York's 16–7 victory would be considered the most important in Super Bowl history. It showed that merging the AFL and NFL made sense.

Namath's pregame guarantee is still talked about today. The lasting image of Super Bowl III, however, is a photo of Broadway Joe jogging off the field, his right index finger in the air.

"Yep, we did it," Namath said. "We did just what we knew we could do and what we said we could do."

Before It Was Super

Vince Lombardi was nervous. That was unusual for the coach of the Green Bay Packers. After all, he had just guided his team to its fourth NFL championship in six years.

Lombardi had seen just about everything in his career. The pressure of big games barely bothered him. But this was different.

The NFL had begun in 1920. The champion was crowned in different ways during the league's first four and a half decades. The NFL Championship Game determined the winner from 1933 to 1966.

Legendary Green Bay Packers coach Vince Lombardi poses with Hall of Fame quarterback Bart Starr in 1967. They won the first two Super Bowls together.

"The Greatest Game"

Until the late 1950s, college football was more popular in the United States than the NFL. Baseball was the national pastime. But one game helped turn professional football into the top sport in America. On December 28, 1958, at Yankee Stadium in New York, the Baltimore Colts and New York Giants faced off in the NFL Championship Game.

The game featured 17 future Hall of Famers. Until then, no NFL Championship Game had gone to overtime. But this one did when Colts quarterback Johnny Unitas drove his team 73 yards in the final minutes. With seven seconds remaining, Steve Myhra's field goal tied it.

The Giants got the ball to begin overtime. They barely missed a first down and punted. Unitas then marched Baltimore downfield. Running back Alan Ameche ran in from the 1-yard line with 8:15 gone for the 23–17 win. The next day, it was being called "The Greatest Game Ever Played."

The league felt it needed to make a change for the 1966 season, though.

A new league called the AFL formed in 1960. Many wrote the AFL off at first. Yet soon it was looking like a real competitor to the NFL. The two leagues often fought over players. Many in the NFL were bitter. They saw the AFL as a weaker league and a nuisance. But some in the NFL believed the AFL was becoming a real threat. The only option, they believed, was to merge.

Owners from the two leagues discussed a merger for months. Some of their meetings were held in secret. Finally, in 1966, they had an agreement. The leagues would stay separate until 1970. Beginning in 1966, however, the two league champions would meet in a true championship game.

It was decided that NFL commissioner Pete Rozelle would keep his job when the leagues merged. He played a major role in planning this championship game. Rozelle decided the site of the title game should be a warm-weather city rather than one team's home stadium. The game would be called the AFL-NFL World Championship Game. And it would take place in Los Angeles on January 15, 1967. All of that had made Lombardi nervous.

A True Championship?

Like most coaches, Lombardi liked to be in control of everything. But this was a new time in professional football. Many on the Packers felt they had won the league title two weeks earlier. They beat the Dallas Cowboys 34–27 in the NFL Championship Game.

Now the Packers had to face the AFL-champion Kansas City Chiefs. Green Bay was heavily favored. After all, most considered the NFL to be superior. But that is what made Lombardi nervous.

"Lombardi got calls from virtually everyone in the NFL saying we were representing the NFL and the pride of the NFL and we couldn't be beaten," Packers guard Jerry Kramer said.

Lombardi was one who felt the Packers had already won the title. He knew of the NFL's rich tradition. Its teams had built a long and storied history. The AFL, meanwhile, was only seven years old. Its teams were mostly in cities that the NFL ignored. People mocked it as "the other league" or even the "Mickey Mouse League."

But Lombardi knew his team's season would be defined by this game. And it bothered him so much that, according to broadcaster Frank Gifford, Lombardi was shaking during a pregame interview.

Game 1

Luckily for Lombardi, there was good reason why his team was favored. The Packers were loaded with veteran talent. Among the Green Bay players that season were future Hall of Famers such as quarterback Bart Starr, running backs Paul Hornung and Jim Taylor, linebacker Ray Nitschke, and offensive linemen Jim Ringo and Forrest Gregg.

Mike Garrett of the AFL's Kansas City Chiefs carries the ball against the NFL's Green Bay Packers in the first AFL-NFL World Championship Game in January 1967.

The Packers could beat teams with a powerful running game or a dangerous pass game. They had a strong, physical defense. Against Kansas City, Green Bay also had a secret weapon.

Backup receiver Max McGee did not expect to play in the Super Bowl. He had just four catches all season. So he was sitting on the sideline at the beginning of the game. But on the sixth play, starter Boyd Dowler went down with a right shoulder injury.

BEFORE IT WAS SUPER

The 34-year-old McGee had to borrow a teammate's helmet after leaving his in the locker room. Then he scored the first touchdown in Super Bowl history on a 37-yard pass from Starr. Later, McGee added a 13-yard touchdown catch. Lombardi could finally relax after that. The Packers were up by 18 points. They added another touchdown for a 35–10 victory. Green Bay had done its job to hold up the honor of the NFL.

Game 2

Lombardi was more relaxed before the next AFL-NFL World Championship Game. The Packers had outlasted the Cowboys 21–17 to win the NFL title. It was known as the "Ice Bowl." The frigid conditions at Lambeau Field in Green Bay that day left some players with frostbite.

The Packers did not have to worry about the cold at the Super Bowl in Miami. Green Bay was nearing the end of its dynasty by then. Nine Packers players had been with the team since Lombardi's first season in 1959. Even Lombardi was wearing down. Though he had not announced it yet, he was planning to step down as coach after playing the Oakland Raiders in what is now known as Super Bowl II.

Green Bay's final game with Lombardi as coach was one of its best. The Packers' defense shut down a Raiders offense that had ripped through the AFL. The Packers forced three fumbles and an interception on defense. Future Hall of Fame cornerback Herb Adderley ran back an

Green Bay Packers running back Donny Anderson steps over the goal line for a touchdown against the Oakland Raiders in Super Bowl II.

interception 60 yards for a score. The offense ran like a machine. McGee, this time knowing where his helmet was, added a 35-yard catch that set up a touchdown. Don Chandler also booted four field goals. Green Bay ran away in the second half to claim a 33–14 win.

The Green Bay players carried Lombardi off the Orange Bowl field for the final time. He understood better than anyone how important those two Super Bowl victories were for his team and his league. Maybe he also sensed the tide was about to change.

New Dynasties

The NFL's dominance ended in the first game officially known as the Super Bowl. The AFL's New York Jets won Super Bowl III. Then the Kansas City Chiefs won Super Bowl IV. Being affiliated with the AFL was no longer an embarrassment. It was good timing, because the two leagues officially merged after that in 1970.

Three NFL teams—the Pittsburgh Steelers, Cleveland Browns, and Baltimore Colts— joined the 10 AFL teams to become the American Football Conference (AFC). Meanwhile, the remaining NFL teams became

Dallas Cowboys quarterback Roger Staubach tosses the ball to a running back during Super Bowl VI against the Miami Dolphins in January 1972.

part of the National Football Conference (NFC). The AFC and NFC still make up the NFL.

The Colts won the AFC in the first season with mixed schedules. Then they took the Super Bowl title in a sloppy 16–13 win over the Dallas Cowboys. The game was decided on Jim O'Brien's 32-yard field goal with five seconds remaining. It was the first Super Bowl with a tight ending. There would be many more.

Super Bowl VI, however, was a blowout. The Cowboys again represented the NFC. And this time they routed the Miami Dolphins 24–3. The people who believed the old NFL was dominant had some talking points. They pointed out that four of the six Super Bowl winners were either NFL teams or former NFL teams.

Those fans of the old NFL would have to quiet down very soon. And they would not have much to say for quite a few years.

Dolphin Dominance

The 1972 Miami Dolphins entered the playoffs with a 14–0 record. No team in the Super Bowl era had previously gone undefeated.

The Dolphins were tested along the way. They had to get past quarterback Terry Bradshaw and the Pittsburgh Steelers in the AFC Championship Game that year. Bradshaw and the Steelers would soon form one of the NFL's strongest dynasties. But 1972 was all about the

Dolphins. They beat Pittsburgh 21–17. Then they moved on to play the Washington Redskins in Super Bowl VII in Los Angeles.

The most famous play of that Super Bowl gave the Redskins their only points. Dolphins kicker Garo Yepremian lined up for a 41-yard field goal, but it was blocked. Yepremian had been a soccer player. He did not usually use his hands while playing sports. But he scooped up the ball and tried to throw a pass on this play. Instead he fumbled the ball directly to Washington's Mike Bass. Bass then ran 49 yards to score.

"I thought I was doing something good, something to help the team," Yepremian said. "Instead it was almost a tragedy. I almost caused a disaster."

It was not a disaster, however. The Dolphins won 14–7. Through 2012, no other team in the Super Bowl era had gone undefeated and won the Super Bowl. The 2007 New England Patriots came close. They went undefeated through the regular season and playoffs before losing in the Super Bowl.

The Dolphins were not quite finished, either. At the end of the 1973 season, the Dolphins became the first team to make three Super Bowls in a row. And Miami won it again. The Dolphins did not go undefeated this time. They lost twice during the regular season. But the Dolphins took down the Minnesota Vikings 24–7. Miami's three-headed running attack of Super Bowl MVP Larry Csonka, Jim Kiick, and Mercury Morris led the way.

America's Team and the Steel Curtain

Those two Miami wins began a string of AFC dominance. Pittsburgh won four Super Bowls and Oakland

Great Coaches

Don Shula. Tom Landry. Chuck Noll. Bud Grant. John Madden. All of these Hall of Fame coaches made their marks during Super Bowls in the 1970s. All of them led their teams to Super Bowls, although Grant lost in all four of his trips with the Minnesota Vikings.

Shula became the winningest coach in professional football history. He guided the Miami Dolphins to two championships. His 1972 team finished off the only perfect season in NFL history through 2012 by winning Super Bowl VII. Noll is the only coach to win four Super Bowl rings through 2011. He took the Pittsburgh Steelers to the top in the 1975, 1976, 1979, and 1980 games. His teams twice beat Landry's Dallas Cowboys. But Landry did capture titles in the 1972 and 1978 contests, beating Shula in 1972. Madden's Oakland Raiders handed Grant and the Vikings their fourth Super Bowl defeat in eight seasons in 1977.

one during the decade. The only team to come through for the NFC was Dallas in 1978. Meanwhile, NFC power Minnesota flopped in all four of its Super Bowl appearances from 1970 to 1977.

The Cowboys provided a bright spot for the NFC during the 1970s. They beat Miami in Super Bowl VI in 1972. Then quarterback Roger Staubach, running back Tony Dorsett, and defensive lineman Randy White led the team to victory in Super Bowl XII in 1978. "America's Team" also represented the NFC in 1976 and 1979. However, the 1970s unquestionably belonged to Pittsburgh's "Steel Curtain."

Pittsburgh built its team through the draft. Bradshaw, running back Franco Harris, wide receiver Lynn Swann, and defensive tackle "Mean" Joe Greene were key first-rounders. Linebackers Jack Ham and Jack Lambert were second-rounders. All later went on to be inducted into the Pro Football Hall of Fame.

The Steelers had a steady offense. They were a running team for their first two Super Bowl victories, in 1975 and 1976. Then they became more of a passing club for their 1979 and 1980 wins.

However, the unmovable Steel Curtain defense really set the team apart. If Greene and his defensive linemates were not overpowering opponents, Lambert and Ham were punishing them with heavy hits. Or Mel Blount and the secondary picked off passes.

Pittsburgh Steelers wide receiver John Stallworth goes up for a catch in Super Bowl XIII against the Dallas Cowboys in January 1979.

The Steelers could beat teams in low-scoring games. Their first two Super Bowl wins were 16–6 over Minnesota and 21–17 over Dallas. And they could outshoot teams. That is what they did to the Cowboys 35–31 in Super Bowl XIII and to the Los Angeles Rams 31–19 the next year.

Several polls have called the 1970s Steelers the NFL's greatest dynasty. Ten Steelers from that era later went into the Pro Football Hall of Fame, including coach Chuck Noll. But soon a pretty good West Coast dynasty would make a strong argument for the best ever, too.

New Powers

S uper Bowls of the 1980s and early 1990s were about changes. The Pittsburgh Steelers made one last stand in 1979. The Steel Curtain defense was already showing holes, though. A great offense, rather than a great defense, led Pittsburgh to Super Bowl XIV in January 1980. In fact, the team featured five future Hall of Famers on offense. They were quarterback Terry Bradshaw, running back Franco Harris, wide receivers Lynn Swann and John Stallworth, and center Mike Webster.

The Steel Curtain came down after quarterback Terry Bradshaw led the Pittsburgh Steelers to their fourth Super Bowl victory in January 1980.

Strike

A peaceful run since the AFL-NFL merger ended with labor unrest in the 1980s and something very new: two player strikes. Coincidentally, the Washington Redskins won the Super Bowl after both the 1982 and the 1987 work stoppages.

The 1982 strike lasted 57 days and cost each team seven regular-season games. There were no byes during the season. The top eight teams in each conference made the playoffs. In Super Bowl XVII, the Redskins beat the Miami Dolphins 27–17.

Five years later, the players went on strike again. This time the league lost only one regular-season game. Replacement players filled in for three weeks of games. Some of the regular players began to return to their teams even as the strike continued. The union ended its walkout after one month. Washington went 3–0 in replacement games, helping it to an 11–4 record. The Redskins then routed the Denver Broncos 42–10 in Super Bowl XXII.

The Steel Curtain era ended with a narrow victory over the Los Angeles Rams in Super Bowl XIV. The game was played at the Rose Bowl, near the Rams' home stadium. But Bradshaw threw three interceptions. Los Angeles took a 19–17 lead into the fourth quarter. However, a late 73-yard touchdown pass to Stallworth gave Pittsburgh the lead in a 31–19 win. It was the Steelers' fourth Super Bowl title in six years. But it was also their last for more than two decades.

"Imagine yourself sitting on top of a great thoroughbred horse," Bradshaw said. "You sit up there and you just feel that power. That's what it was like, playing quarterback on that team. It was a great ride."

Black Hole

A new AFC team with black uniforms emerged. The Oakland Raiders took the Super Bowl title after the 1980 season with a cast of characters straight out of the movies. Those Raiders loved to play football. They also had a reputation for being renegades. So the setting of New Orleans was perfect for the likes of characters such as linebacker Ted Hendricks and defensive lineman John Matuszak.

On the other sideline were the Philadelphia Eagles. Eagles coach Dick Vermeil was uptight about nearly everything during Super Bowl week. His players played nervously and were routed 27–10.

A New Dynasty

The Bay Area of California celebrated another Super Bowl title the next year. But it was no celebration for the Raiders. Instead the San Francisco 49ers ruled the NFL for much of the later part of the decade.

The 49ers had joined the NFL in 1950. Until 1981, they had only made the playoffs four times and never been to a Super Bowl. Their playoff campaign that year almost fell short, too. San Francisco trailed the Dallas Cowboys 27–21 in the final minutes of the 1982 NFC title game.

Then quarterback Joe Montana marched the 49ers to the Dallas 6-yard line. On third down, he was supposed to throw to wide receiver Freddie Solomon. But Solomon slipped. So Montana rolled right and threw high toward the back of the end zone. He knew the pass would either be incomplete or receiver Dwight Clark would soar high to snag it. But the ball seemed to be thrown too high as Clark leaped.

"I couldn't really see him," Clark said of Montana, "but I saw the ball coming to me. I thought, 'Man, that's high.' People don't know this, but I kind of made a double catch on it. I stopped it in the air and then caught it on the way down."

Touchdown. The famous play would forever be known in San Francisco as "The Catch." It sent the 49ers to their first Super Bowl. And the 49ers then defeated the Cincinnati Bengals for their first championship. The game was not without some drama, though.

San Francisco appeared to have the game locked up early. The 49ers took a 20–0 lead into halftime. But Cincinnati, also in its first Super Bowl, came fighting back. The Bengals closed to within 20–14. But San Francisco held on from there. A new dynasty had begun.

Dwight Clark's "The Catch" in the NFC Championship Game after the 1981 season ushered in a new era of dominance for the San Francisco 49ers.

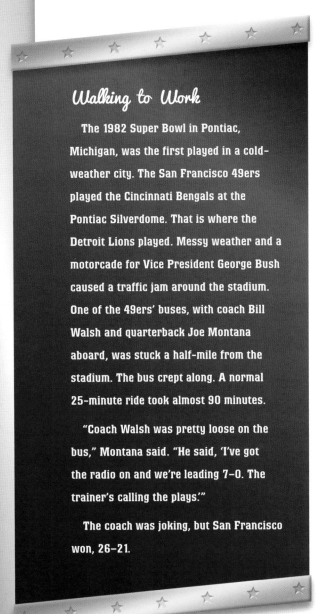

Walking to Work

The 1982 Super Bowl in Pontiac, Michigan, was the first played in a cold-weather city. The San Francisco 49ers played the Cincinnati Bengals at the Pontiac Silverdome. That is where the Detroit Lions played. Messy weather and a motorcade for Vice President George Bush caused a traffic jam around the stadium. One of the 49ers' buses, with coach Bill Walsh and quarterback Joe Montana aboard, was stuck a half-mile from the stadium. The bus crept along. A normal 25-minute ride took almost 90 minutes.

"Coach Walsh was pretty loose on the bus," Montana said. "He said, 'I've got the radio on and we're leading 7–0. The trainer's calling the plays.'"

The coach was joking, but San Francisco won, 26–21.

The 49ers won three more Super Bowls after the 1984, 1988, and 1989 seasons. After defenses had dominated the NFL for years, San Francisco dominated with a powerful offense. Coach Bill Walsh was known for his West Coast offense. It featured more passing than most NFL offenses.

The 49ers had just the right men to run that offense. Montana was named MVP in three of those four Super Bowls. Wide receiver Jerry Rice was MVP in Super Bowl XXIII after the 1988 season. Rice went on to set several receiving records. In 2010 the NFL Network named him the league's best player ever. The 49ers averaged 34.8 points in those four Super Bowl victories.

Washington Redskins quarterback Doug Williams looks downfield for a receiver during Super Bowl XXII in January 1988.

More Power

Like Walsh, Washington Redskins coach Joe Gibbs was a great offensive coach. Through 2012, Gibbs remained the only coach to win three Super Bowls with three different starting quarterbacks. One of those quarterbacks was Doug Williams. He led the Redskins to victory over the Denver Broncos in Super Bowl XXII in 1988. Williams threw for 340 yards and four touchdowns in the game. More importantly, he became the first African-American quarterback to win a Super Bowl title.

The story on the other side was not so happy. The loss was Denver's second in three tries during the 1980s. The Broncos had lost the previous year to the New York Giants and also lost in the 1990 game.

Commercials

Over the years, the Super Bowl has become almost an unofficial national holiday. Millions of people come together each year to watch the game. Eventually, many people began watching for the commercials as well. Since so many people were watching the Super Bowl, advertisers found it was a prime time to make memorable commercials. One of the most famous was a 1984 commercial introducing Apple's Macintosh personal computer. Other famous commercials from the 1980s included Budweiser's Bud Bowl; Michael J. Fox and the Pepsi Robot; Wendy's "Where's The Beef?"; and Coca-Cola's 3-D ad.

Many great teams won Super Bowls during the 1980s. The most dominant of those might have been the 1985 Chicago Bears. Coach Mike Ditka and defensive coordinator Buddy Ryan put together an immovable unit. It allowed only 198 points in 16 regular-season games. That was 65 fewer than anyone else.

The Bears nearly went undefeated. Only the Miami Dolphins were able to beat them during the regular season. The Bears were 12–0 when they met. But a 38–24 Miami win kept the 1972 Dolphins as the NFL's only perfect team to that point. Chicago continued to roll, though. The Bears finished 15–1. Then they shut out the Giants and Rams in the playoffs. The dominant season ended with a 46–10 win over the New England Patriots in Super Bowl XX.

One of Chicago's heaviest players was defensive tackle William Perry. He was nicknamed "Refrigerator" because he was as big as one. He also could move. The Bears even used him at running back for some plays. Perry actually ran for a one-yard touchdown in the Super Bowl. Meanwhile, Chicago's superstar running back Walter Payton was kept out of the end zone in the game.

The Bears even came up with a song and dance to celebrate their greatness. They unveiled the "Super Bowl Shuffle" well before they beat the Patriots.

"I guess the great thing about our 'Shuffle' was that it brought the city together," said wide receiver Willie Gault. "It brought fun back to the league."

Chapter 5

The High-Flying 1990s

The 1989 San Francisco 49ers won the team's fourth championship in nine seasons. The result was one of the most lopsided victories in Super Bowl history. The 49ers beat the Denver Broncos 55–10 on January 28, 1990. San Francisco quarterback Joe Montana became the only three-time Super Bowl MVP. He set a Super Bowl record with five touchdown passes. Meanwhile, the loss was the Broncos' fourth in four Super Bowl appearances.

Quarterback Joe Montana looks for a receiver in Super Bowl XXIV. His San Francisco 49ers won their fourth Super Bowl that year over the Denver Broncos.

George Seifert had taken over as 49ers coach in 1989. Montana left after the 1992 season. The team remained a force in the NFC, though. New quarterback Steve Young led the 1994 49ers back to the Super Bowl. Then he broke Montana's record with six touchdown passes in a 49–26 romp over the San Diego Chargers on January 29, 1995. Four of those touchdowns were in the first half.

"When we're hitting on all cylinders, I don't think anyone can stop us," Hall of Fame wide receiver Jerry Rice said.

The 49ers' win gave the NFC 11 straight Super Bowl wins. That streak eventually reached 13. The most frequent victim was the Buffalo Bills.

Buffalo Woes

"Is our goal to win?" Buffalo coach Marv Levy once asked. "No! Our goal is to develop our team, to earn what we get, to learn, to develop unselfish attitudes. If we achieve that, the result is that we'll win."

The Bills certainly won games. They won 49 regular-season games between 1990 and 1993 while losing only 15. There was one game they could not win, though: the Super Bowl.

First came a game defined by two words: "Wide Right." The Bills met the New York Giants in Super Bowl XXV on January 27, 1991. Buffalo came into the game with a powerful offense. But the Giants kept the Bills' offense off the field for more than 40 minutes.

Buffalo Bills

The Buffalo Bills went down in history as the only team to lose four straight Super Bowls. And they remained the only one through 2012. So it is easy to forget that the Bills had to be a pretty good team to reach four consecutive Super Bowls in the first place. Through 2012, they were the only team to do that, too.

After trailing 12–3, New York rallied to lead 20–19. Still, Buffalo had a shot. Bills quarterback Jim Kelly marched his team down the field as the game neared its end. He got his team close enough to attempt a field goal on the last play. But kicker Scott Norwood's 47-yard try went wide to the right.

"Wide right," Giants star linebacker Lawrence Taylor shouted. "Love those two words."

The Bills returned to the Super Bowl the next year. This one was not very close, though. The game got off to a bad start for Buffalo. Star running back Thurman Thomas could not find his helmet and missed the first play. It did not get much better after that.

The Washington Redskins forced five turnovers in a 37–24 victory. And then along came "the Triplets."

America's Team Again

The Dallas Cowboys had once been awful. They went just 1–15 in 1989 in quarterback Troy Aikman's rookie season. But the team continued to build through the draft. Soon it had three star first-round picks leading the offense: Aikman, running back Emmitt Smith, and wide receiver Michael Irvin. The three became known as "the Triplets." And all three players later made the Pro Football Hall of Fame.

The Cowboys had reached four Super Bowls and won two of them, but their last appearance had been in 1979. They did not reach the big game again until 1993. The opposing Buffalo Bills had dominated the AFC and returned to the Super Bowl for the third straight year. And they lost in the Super Bowl for a third straight year.

This defeat was embarrassing from the beginning. The Bills never looked ready to play in a 52–17 loss. Dallas forced a Super Bowl-record nine turnovers in the game. One of those nearly made the game more lopsided. Dallas defensive tackle Leon Lett picked up a fumble and headed toward the goal line. He thought he was in the clear. So just before he reached the goal line, he held out the ball in his right hand in an early celebration of his touchdown. Except Bills receiver Don Beebe had raced after Lett. Beebe knocked the ball loose and through the end zone,

Dallas Cowboys quarterback Troy Aikman hands off to running back Emmitt Smith during the Cowboys' win over the Buffalo Bills in Super Bowl XXVII.

giving the ball back to Buffalo. It was about the only thing that went right for the Bills.

The two teams met once again in Super Bowl XXVIII the next year. Dallas' 30–13 victory tied "America's Team" with the Pittsburgh Steelers and San Francisco 49ers with four Super Bowl titles. That record stood for just one season, as Young led the 49ers to a fifth victory in 1995. But the Cowboys came back to win a fifth one year after that.

It seemed that nobody could slow down the Triplets when they made it to the big game. In Super Bowl XXX, the Cowboys got their fifth championship by handing Pittsburgh its first Super Bowl defeat, 27–17.

Powers Return

After a down period, the Pittsburgh Steelers were back in the mix for Super Bowls by the mid-1990s. So was another former NFL powerhouse: the Green Bay Packers. Led by quarterback Brett Favre, Green Bay reached Super Bowl XXXI in 1997 and Super Bowl XXXII in 1998.

Super Bowl XXXI was in New Orleans, Louisiana. Favre had grown up in neighboring Mississippi. He got off to a hot start against the New England Patriots. Favre threw a 54-yard touchdown pass to wide receiver Andre Rison early in the game. Then he sprinted all over the field with his helmet off and held high, his face filled with a wide grin.

Favre later had an 81-yard connection with wide receiver Antonio Freeman. Then he ran for a touchdown in the 35–21 victory. The Packers got back to the Super Bowl in 1998 but lost to the Denver Broncos.

Rocky Mountain High, Finally

Brett Favre and the Green Bay Packers won Super Bowl XXXI on January 26, 1997. It was Green Bay's first title since winning Super Bowl I and Super Bowl II in 1967 and 1968. Favre had a Hall of Fame career, but it ended up being his only Super Bowl title. A main reason for that was John Elway.

The Denver Broncos' quarterback had suffered one-sided defeats in the 1987, 1988, and 1990 Super Bowls. He was nearing the end of his career in 1997. Then the Broncos made the playoffs as a wild card and surged all the way to the Super Bowl in January 1998.

Denver Broncos quarterback John Elway celebrates after leading his team to victory over the Green Bay Packers in Super Bowl XXXII in January 1998.

Still, not much was expected from Denver. Most favored the Packers to win again. In fact, the Broncos had become the punch line to many football jokes, just as the Bills had been. But Elway and running back Terrell Davis put an end to those jokes.

Davis ran for 157 yards. But the biggest play came in the third quarter. The Broncos had a third down with the game tied 17–17. Elway scrambled. As he leaped in the air trying to get a first down, he was hit in the legs by a Packers safety. Another Packer then hit him higher, and Elway twirled around like a helicopter. When he landed, he had the first down. Soon after, Denver took the lead in a 31–24 victory.

"This wipes away all the losses," Elway said. "I guarantee you, it's 10 times better than anything I could imagine."

Elway tasted victory again the next year over the Atlanta Falcons. He retired after that. He ended his Hall of Fame career on top with two straight Super Bowls wins.

Greatest Show on Turf

The finish of the 2000 Super Bowl was as exciting as they come. The Rams had moved from Los Angeles to St. Louis in 1995. In the 1999 season, they became known as the "Greatest Show on Turf."

The Rams featured a high-powered offense that thrived in St. Louis' domed stadium. The Rams outscored everyone thanks to such stars as running back Marshall Faulk, receivers Isaac Bruce and Torry Holt, and quarterback Kurt Warner. Warner hardly had played a down in the NFL when he became the starter that preseason. But he had an MVP season.

To cap it off the Rams needed to beat the powerful Tennessee Titans. St. Louis had the edge in nearly all of the stats coming into the game. But Tennessee rallied from 16–0 to tie the game.

Warner put the Rams back on top 23–16 with a 73-yard touchdown pass to Bruce with 1:54 left. Tennessee still had time, though. Tennessee quarterback Steve McNair led his team back down the field. The Titans backed the Rams' exhausted defense all the way back to their own

St. Louis Rams linebacker Mike Jones wraps up Tennessee Titans wide receiver Kevin Dyson just short of the end zone to give the Rams the Super Bowl XXXIV title.

10-yard line. Now there was time for just one more play, and it needed to be a touchdown.

McNair hit wide receiver Kevin Dyson at the 5-yard line. As Dyson headed toward the end zone, only Rams linebacker Mike Jones could stop him. And that is exactly what Jones did. With a textbook tackle, Jones took down Dyson as the receiver stretched the ball out with his right arm, trying to get the ball to the goal line. He came up a yard short.

Rams 23, Titans 16.

The Greatest Show on Turf indeed.

A New Generation

In one year, the Super Bowl went from the great offense of the St. Louis Rams to the overpowering defense of the Baltimore Ravens. In four postseason games, the Ravens allowed just 23 points. That included just one offensive touchdown. The New York Giants hardly had a chance in Super Bowl XXXV. The Ravens manhandled them 34–7.

"We had no fear of any offense in the NFL this year," Ravens safety Rod Woodson said. "We wanted shutouts."

Baltimore Ravens linebacker Ray Lewis earned MVP honors at Super Bowl XXXV after a dominant defensive performance.

That's Offensive

New England coach Bill Belichick was known as a defensive master. A key injury in 2001 had given the Patriots a jolt of offense, though. Quarterback Drew Bledsoe was hurt in the second game of the season. A little-known second-year player replaced him. His name was Tom Brady.

The Patriots had started 0–2 under Bledsoe. Behind Brady, they finished 11–3. Only five teams scored more points that season than New England. But at the top of that list were the St. Louis Rams. Behind MVP quarterback Kurt Warner and superstar running back Marshall Faulk, the "Greatest Show on Turf" scored 503 points that season.

The Rams were 14-point favorites when they met the Patriots in Super Bowl XXXVI. But Brady and the Patriots stole the show. On defense, Belichick designed a game plan to stop the Rams. After three quarters, New England led 17–3. Still, the Rams rallied. Warner ran for one touchdown and threw for another. With 1:21 remaining the Patriots got the ball on their 17-yard line. The score was tied. It appeared the first overtime in Super Bowl history was approaching.

Not to Belichick or Brady. Despite having no timeouts, the Patriots' offense took the field. Brady led the Patriots to the Rams' 30 with seven seconds remaining. It all came down to Patriots kicker Adam Vinatieri.

The New England Patriots reach out to touch the Vince Lombardi Trophy after defeating the St. Louis Rams in Super Bowl XXXVI in February 2002.

And as time expired, his 48-yard field goal soared through the uprights to clinch a 20–17 win.

As confetti flew down from the Louisiana Superdome roof, the Patriots celebrated a Super Bowl victory. Brady was named Super Bowl MVP. It was a scene that fans would get used to. Two years later, Brady led the Patriots to a 32–29 victory over the Carolina Panthers in Super Bowl XXVIII. Brady was again the MVP. Vinatieri again sealed the game with a late field goal, this time with four seconds left. Then the Patriots downed the Philadelphia Eagles 24–21 in the next year's Super Bowl. Brady threw for 236 yards and two touchdowns. Patriots receiver Deion Branch was named Super Bowl MVP.

The Dallas Cowboys of the 1990s were the only other team to win three Super Bowls in four years. The Brady-led Patriots of the early-2000s were now in the discussion for the best team in Super Bowl history.

Close games became normal in the next few Super Bowls. The only one-sided games in the decade came in 2003 and 2007. The Tampa Bay Buccaneers beat the Oakland Raiders 48–21 in Super Bowl XXXVII in 2003. The Indianapolis Colts defeated the Chicago Bears 29–17 in Super Bowl XLI four years later.

Pittsburgh Adds One for the Thumb

No single team dominated in the Super Bowl quite like the Patriots had in the years that followed. The Pittsburgh Steelers came close, though. They had won four Super Bowls from 1975 to 1980. They reached the Super Bowl again in 1996 but lost to the Cowboys. The Steelers finally got a fifth Super Bowl title in 2006. Then they won a sixth in 2009.

Pittsburgh beat the Seattle Seahawks 21–10 in Super Bowl XL in 2006. That was Seattle's only Super Bowl appearance since coming into the league in 1976. It was a perfect ending for Pittsburgh's star running back Jerome Bettis. The Super Bowl was in his hometown of Detroit. The man nicknamed "The Bus" was able to ride off into retirement with his only championship ring.

Three years later, the Steelers squeezed past the Arizona Cardinals in Super Bowl XLIII. Wide receiver Larry Fitzgerald scored on a 63-yard touchdown pass to give Arizona a 23–20 lead with just 2:37 remaining. But Steelers quarterback Ben Roethlisberger drove his team back down the field. Then he barely avoided a sack to throw a six-yard pass to triple-covered wide receiver Santonio Holmes in the corner of the end zone. The touchdown with 35 seconds left gave Pittsburgh a record sixth win.

Historic Super Bowl XLI

The Chicago Bears and Indianapolis Colts played a historic Super Bowl XLI in 2007. No African-American coach had led a team to the Super Bowl before that. But both the Colts' Tony Dungy and the Bears' Lovie Smith did just that in 2007. Indianapolis came out on top, 29–17.

It was also a historic win for quarterback Peyton Manning. He had proven to be statistically one of the best quarterbacks of all time. Until 2007, however, he had always fallen short in the playoffs. Now he was Super Bowl MVP. Manning had a chance for another title three years later. This time, however, the once-miserable New Orleans Saints won their first Super Bowl, 31–17.

Peyton Manning was one of three star quarterbacks in his family. His father Archie was an All-American at Mississippi before playing 14 standout professional seasons. Peyton's younger brother Eli Manning led the New York Giants to Super Bowl titles in 2008 and 2012.

Pittsburgh had a chance to win a seventh Super Bowl after the 2010 season. However, quarterback Aaron Rodgers was in the midst of leading the Green Bay Packers back to glory. He led Green Bay to a 31–25 victory.

Perfection Postponed

Brady and the Patriots were the NFL's dominant team during the early 2000s. Two of the most dominant Patriots teams ever came later. But twice the New York Giants ended the Patriots' season on a sour note in the Super Bowl.

Super Bowl XLII in February 2008 was supposed to be a mismatch. With superstar wide receiver Randy Moss in the mix, Brady had set an NFL record with 50 touchdown passes that season.

Pittsburgh Steelers wide receiver Santonio Holmes runs with the ball after making a catch in Super Bowl XLIII in February 2009.

The Patriots went 16–0 in the regular season. Only the 1972 Miami Dolphins, who went 14–0, had gone undefeated in the Super Bowl era. After winning two playoff games, New England just needed to beat the Giants in the Super Bowl to complete the perfect season.

The Patriots had beaten the Giants 38–35 in the final regular-season game. That game proved important for the Giants. They finished only 10–6 and made the playoffs as a wild card. But the close defeat to the Patriots made the Giants believe they could win.

New York won three straight road games to get to the Super Bowl. The Giants were brimming with confidence by then. The players were sure that their strong pass rush and timely offense could handle the undefeated opponent.

That pass rush indeed unnerved Brady. The Giants sacked him five times and hit him a dozen more. Quarterback Eli Manning calmly led the Giants to two fourth-quarter drives for touchdowns. The second one ended with 35 seconds remaining on a 13-yard pass to wide receiver Plaxico Burress for the championship.

That final drive featured a "miracle" catch by backup receiver David Tyree. He trapped the ball against his helmet with one hand as he fell to the ground. Several Patriots stared in disbelief after that catch. They were even more stunned when the Giants had won 17–14.

Many of the 2007 Patriots had left by the 2011 season. Brady and Belichick were still there, though. They led the team to a 13–3 record and back to the Super Bowl. As it turned out, they again met the Giants. And the Giants were again surging.

The game was a chance for redemption after New York ended New England's perfect-season attempt four years earlier. It again ended in heartbreak for Brady and the Patriots, though. After the Patriots led 17–9 in the third quarter, the Giants scored 12 straight points.

New York Giants wide receiver Mario Manningham hauls in an improbable catch late in Super Bowl XLVI. It helped the Giants beat the New England Patriots.

New England still led 17–15 with time winding down. It looked like the Patriots might get another Super Bowl title. Then Manning came through with another historic play. He flung a long pass down the left sideline from his 12. The ball fell perfectly into the outstretched arms of wide receiver Mario Manningham, who was double-covered, for 38 yards.

"Biggest play of my life," Manningham shouted after the game.

Soon the Giants scored a touchdown to take the lead. The Patriots were unable to answer. The Giants had yet another thrilling championship game win. And that is why they call it the *Super* Bowl.

TIMELINE

The NFL's Green Bay Packers beat the AFL's Kansas City Chiefs on January 15 in what is now known as Super Bowl I.

1967

New York Jets quarterback Joe Namath outrageously guarantees a win over the Baltimore Colts before his Jets win 16–7 in Super Bowl III.

1969

The Miami Dolphins complete a perfect season after downing the Washington Redskins 14–7 in Super Bowl VII on January 14.

1973

The Pittsburgh Steelers' "Steel Curtain" dynasty comes to a close with a fourth Super Bowl title in six seasons on January 20.

1980

Quarterback Joe Montana leads the San Francisco 49ers to their first of four Super Bowl titles during the 1980s. Montana is MVP of three of them.

1982

For the first time since Super Bowl II, the Green Bay Packers get back to the big game. They beat the New England Patriots 35–21 on January 26.

1997

After four Super Bowl losses, John Elway and the Denver Broncos edge Green Bay 31–24 to take the title on January 25.

1998

The St. Louis Rams hold on to beat the Tennessee Titans 23–16 when Mike Jones tackles the Titans' Kevin Dyson at the Rams' 1-yard line.

2000

In a stunning upset, New England slows down the Rams' "Greatest Show on Turf" to win 20–17 in Super Bowl XXXVI on February 3.

2002

The Patriots become the second team to win three titles in four years when they beat the Philadelphia Eagles 24–21 in Super Bowl XXXIX.

2005

After a strike-shortened season, the Washington Redskins come through for their first Super Bowl win, beating the Miami Dolphins 27–17.

1983

On January 28, the San Francisco 49ers romp past the Denver Broncos 55–10. The 49ers match the Steelers with four Super Bowl titles.

1990

The Buffalo Bills lose a fourth straight Super Bowl by falling to the Dallas Cowboys 30–13. No other team through 2012 has played in even three straight.

1994

The 49ers score right away and do not stop in a 49–26 rout over the San Diego Chargers on January 29 for their fifth Super Bowl win.

1995

The Dallas Cowboys become the second team to win five Super Bowls after downing the Steelers 27–17 on January 28.

1996

The Steelers win their first Super Bowl since 1980 with a 21–10 win over the Seattle Seahawks. They become the first team to win six Super Bowls.

2006

Peyton Manning finally wins a Super Bowl and also takes the MVP honors as his Indianapolis Colts beat the Chicago Bears 29–17 in Super Bowl XLI.

2007

David Tyree makes a "miracle" catch and the New York Giants shock the undefeated Patriots 17–14 in Super Bowl XLII on February 3.

2008

The New Orleans Saints, a league doormat for decades, win their first title, beating the Colts 31–17 on February 7 in Super Bowl XLIV.

2010

The Giants pull off another upset over the Patriots. This time the Giants win 21–17 on February 5 to claim their fourth Super Bowl title.

2012

CHAMPIONSHIP OVERVIEW

The Trophy

The Vince Lombardi Trophy was named in 1970 after the legendary Green Bay Packers coach. Made by Tiffany & Co., the trophy stands 22 inches tall, weighs 7 pounds, and is worth about $25,000.

The Legends

Troy Aikman, Michael Irvin, Emmitt Smith (Dallas Cowboys): The Triplets led the Cowboys to three Super Bowl titles in four years during the 1990s.

Terry Bradshaw (Pittsburgh Steelers): With help from the "Steel Curtain" defense, the quarterback led his team to four Super Bowl titles from 1975 to 1980, twice as MVP.

Tom Brady (New England Patriots): The quarterback led his team to five Super Bowls between 2002 and 2012, winning three, twice as MVP.

Joe Montana (San Francisco 49ers): The quarterback led the 49ers to four Super Bowls from 1982 to 1990, three times as MVP.

The Victors

Pittsburgh Steelers: six (1975, 1976, 1979, 1980, 2006, 2009)

Dallas Cowboys: five (1972, 1978, 1993, 1994, 1996)

San Francisco 49ers: five (1982, 1985, 1989, 1990, 1995)

GLOSSARY

draft
A system used by professional sports leagues to select new players in order to spread incoming talent among all teams. The NFL Draft is held each April.

dynasty
A team that wins many championships over a short period of time.

merge
To unite into a single body.

retired
When one has officially ended his career.

rivals
Opponents that bring out great emotion in one another's fans and players.

rookie
A player's first year in the NFL.

strike
A work stoppage by employees in protest of working conditions.

West Coast Offense
A passing attack designed by San Francisco 49ers coach Bill Walsh in the 1970s that still is used today.

FOR MORE INFORMATION

Selected Bibliography

Garner, Joe. *100 Yards of Glory*. New York: Houghton Mifflin Harcourt
   Publishing, 2011.

McGinn, Bob. *The Ultimate Super Bowl Book*. Minneapolis, MN: MVP Books,
   2009.

Rappoport, Ken. *The Little League That Could*. Lanham, MD: Taylor Trade
   Publishing, 2010.

Further Readings

Christopher, Matt. *The Super Bowl: Legendary Sports Events*. New York:
   Little, Brown and Company, 2009.

Doeden, Matt. *Tom Brady*. Minneapolis, MN: Twenty-First Century Books,
   2009.

The Football Book: Expanded Edition. New York: Sports Illustrated, 2009.

Web Links

To learn more about the Super Bowl, visit ABDO Publishing Company online at **www.abdopublishing.com**. Web sites about the Super Bowl are featured on our Book Links page. These links are routinely monitored and updated to provide the most current information available.

Place to Visit

Pro Football Hall of Fame
2121 George Halas Dr., NW
Canton, OH 44708
(330) 456-8207
www.profootballhof.com
This hall of fame and museum highlights the greatest players and moments in the history of the National Football League. Terry Bradshaw, Joe Montana, and coach Vince Lombardi are among the people enshrined. A new class is enshrined prior to each NFL season. The celebration includes an NFL exhibition game. The Lamar Hunt Super Bowl Gallery at the Hall of Fame chronicles the history and stars of each Super Bowl through artifacts and interactive exhibits.

INDEX

About the Author

Barry Wilner has been a sportswriter for the Associated Press since 1976. He has covered every Super Bowl since 1985 and other major events. Wilner has written several books and teaches journalism at Manhattanville College. He and his wife have four children and one grandchild.